WITHDRAWN

D1192708

States

MISSOURI

by Jordan Mills

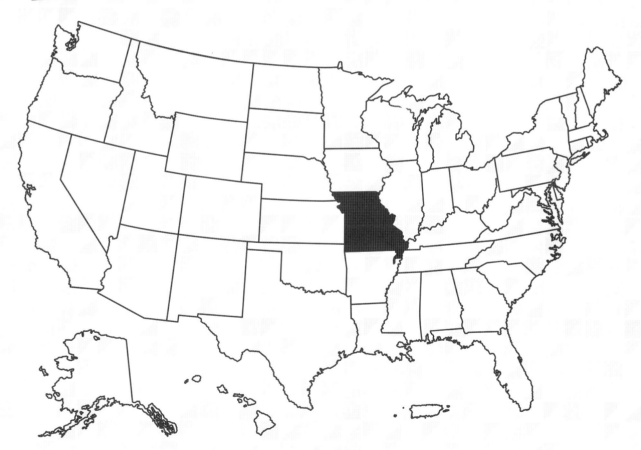

CAPSTONE PRESS
a capstone imprint

Next Page Books are published by Capstone Press,
1710 Roe Crest Drive, North Mankato, Minnesota 56003
www.mycapstone.com

Copyright © 2017 by Capstone Press, a Capstone imprint. All rights
reserved. No part of this publication may be reproduced in whole or
in part, or stored in a retrieval system, or transmitted in any form
or by any means, electronic, mechanical, photocopying, recording, or
otherwise, without written permission of the publisher.

Library of Congress Cataloging-in-Publication Data
Cataloging-in-publication information is on file with the Library of
Congress.
ISBN 978-1-5157-0412-6 (library binding)
ISBN 978-1-5157-0471-3 (paperback)
ISBN 978-1-5157-0523-9 (ebook PDF)

Editorial Credits
Jaclyn Jaycox, editor; Kazuko Collins and Katy LaVigne, designers;
Morgan Walters, media researcher; Laura Manthe, production specialist

Photo Credits
Alamy: Tom Uhlman, 7; Capstone Press: Angi Gahler, map 4, 7;
Corbis: Bettmann, top 19; CriaImages.com: Jay Robert Nash Collection,
bottom 19; Dreamstime: Bonita Cheshier, top right 21; Getty Images:
JeremyMasonMcGraw.com, 11; Glow Images: Craig Aurness/CORBIS,
10; iStockphoto: Lokibaho, 16; Library of Congress: C.M. Bell, 25,
Prints and Photographs Division Washington, D.C., 28; Newscom:
akg-images, top 18, Ken Welsh, 12, Picture History, middle 18, 27,
ZUMAPRESS/KEYSTONE Pictures USA, bottom 18; North Wind
Picture Archives, 26; One Mile Up, Inc., flag, seal 23; Shutterstock:
aceshot1, bottom left 8, amolson7, cover, 9, arhendrix, 14, Chantelle
Bosch, middle right 21, Christian Davidson, bottom right 8, Daniel
Prudek, bottom left 21, Dustie, 29, Featureflash, middle 19, Fotokostic,
15, Jothi Pallikkathayil, 6, Krabikus, top 24, Mara Popa, top right
20, Melinda Fawver, bottom right 21, MP cz, bottom right 20, Nagel
Photography, 13, Nerthuz, middle left 21, R. Gino Santa Maria, bottom
24, Rudy Balasko, 5, Semmick Photo, bottom left 20, top left 21,
StevenRussellSmithPhotos, top left 20, TommyBrison, 17

All design elements by Shutterstock

Printed and bound in China.
0316/CA21600187
012016   009436F16

TABLE OF CONTENTS

Want to take your research further? Ask your librarian if your school subscribes to PebbleGo Next. If so, when you see this helpful symbol 🖱 throughout the book, log onto www.pebblegonext.com for bonus downloads and information.

LOCATION

Located in the central United States, Missouri borders eight states. To its west lie Nebraska and Kansas. Oklahoma sits to the southwest. Arkansas lies to Missouri's south. The eastern border is shared with Illinois, Kentucky, and Tennessee. Iowa is north of Missouri. Missouri's capital, Jefferson City, is on the Missouri River. Kansas City, St. Louis, and Springfield are the state's biggest cities.

PebbleGo Next Bonus!
To print and label your own map, go to www.pebblegonext.com and search keywords: MO MAP

About 318,000 people live in St. Louis.

GEOGRAPHY

Missouri's landscape includes plains, hills, and rivers. The flat land of the Osage Plains is in western Missouri. In northern Missouri lies the Dissected Till Plains area, which is hillier than the Osage Plains. The St. Francois Mountains are in southeast Missouri. The state's highest point, Taum Sauk Mountain, is found in this mountain range. It rises 1,772 feet (540 meters) above sea level.

Two of the nation's largest rivers flow through Missouri. The Mississippi River creates Missouri's eastern border. The Missouri River forms part of the state's northwestern border and flows east across the middle of Missouri.

PebbleGo Next Bonus! To watch a video about Missouri's main attractions, go to www.pebblegonext.com and search keywords: **MO VIDEO**

The Lake of the Ozarks has more than 1,150 miles (1,851 kilometers) of shoreline.

These natural rock formations are found on Taum Sauk Mountain, the highest elevation in Missouri.

WEATHER

Missouri's climate is generally mild. The summer temperature averages 76 degrees Fahrenheit (24 degrees Celsius). During winter, the average temperature is 32°F (0°C).

Average High and Low Temperatures (Jefferson City, MO)

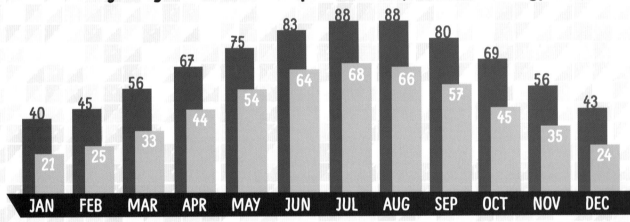

	JAN	FEB	MAR	APR	MAY	JUN	JUL	AUG	SEP	OCT	NOV	DEC
High	40	45	56	67	75	83	88	88	80	69	56	43
Low	21	25	33	44	54	64	68	66	57	45	35	24

LANDMARKS

Gateway Arch

St. Louis' Gateway Arch is the tallest monument built in the United States. It stands 630 feet (192 m) high.

Pony Express Museum

In St. Joseph people can visit the Pony Express Museum. The Pony Express was a mail service that ran from 1860 to 1861. Men rode horses carrying saddlebags of mail between St. Joseph and Sacramento, California. Delivery time was about 10 days.

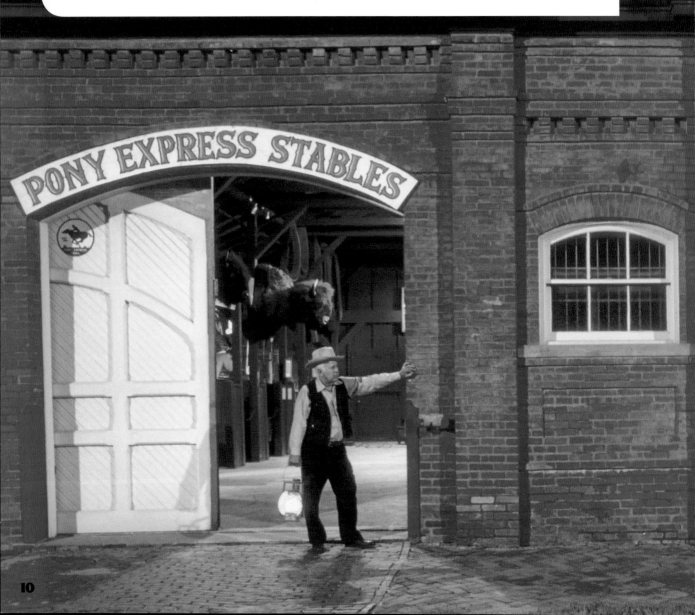

Branson

Millions of visitors come to the city of Branson in the Ozark Mountains in southwest Missouri each year. The city features more than 90 music and variety shows.

Explorer René-Robert Cavelier set sail down the Mississippi River in 1682. He claimed land, including the Missouri area, for his home country of France.

More than 1,500 years ago, Missouri was home to native people known as the Mound Builders. By the 1600s, the Sauk, Fox, Iowa, and Osage Indians lived in Missouri. French explorers Jacques Marquette and Louis Jolliet arrived in Missouri in 1673. In 1682 Frenchman René-Robert Cavelier, known as Sieur de la Salle, claimed a large region, including Missouri, for France. In 1803 France sold Louisiana to the United States. In the early 1800s, U.S. citizens settled in the Missouri area. Missouri became the 24th U.S. state in 1821.

Missouri's state government has three branches. The governor leads the executive branch, which carries out laws. The legislature is made up of the 34-member Senate and the 163-member House of Representatives. They make the laws for Missouri. Judges and their courts make up the judicial branch.

The Missouri Judiciary is made up of three levels of courts: trial, appellate, and the Supreme Court of Missouri.

INDUSTRY

Missouri's economy depends on agriculture, service industries, and manufacturing. Most Missourians have jobs in service industries. Some of these people work in tourism, government, retail, education, banking, or health care.

> Aerospace and automobile manufacturing are two of the state's top industries.

About two-thirds of Missouri is farmland. Soybeans are the state's most valuable crop. More than half of Missouri's farm income is from livestock. Farmers raise poultry, hogs, cattle, and sheep.

Manufacturing has been an important industry in Missouri for many years. Missourians manufacture aircraft, automobiles, pet food, motorcycles, electronic equipment, and chemicals. Food processing is also an important part of the Missouri economy. Large plants in Kansas City turn wheat into flour. The nation's largest beer manufacturing company, Anheuser-Busch in St. Louis, processes grain to make beer.

Soybeans can be used to make a variety of items including carpet backing and insulation.

POPULATION

Most Missourians have European backgrounds. About 5 million white people live in the state. Many Germans settled in the state in the 1800s. People of Italian, French, English, and Irish descent are also well represented in the state. African-Americans are the second-largest ethnic group of Missouri. About 700,000 African-Americans live in the state. About 220,000 people in Missouri are Hispanic. Asians have lived in Missouri since before the 1860s. Asians compose less than 2 percent of Missouri's population. American Indians make up less than 1 percent of the state's residents.

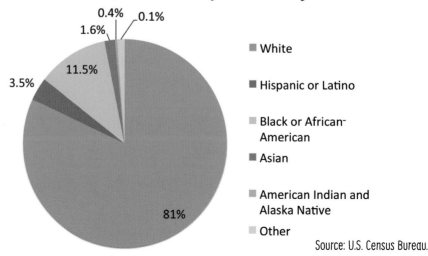

Population by Ethnicity

- 0.4%
- 0.1%
- 1.6%
- 11.5%
- 3.5%
- 81%

- White
- Hispanic or Latino
- Black or African-American
- Asian
- American Indian and Alaska Native
- Other

Source: U.S. Census Bureau.

FAMOUS PEOPLE

George Washington Carver
(circa 1864–1943) was a scientist at Tuskegee Institute in Alabama. He developed hundreds of new products from peanuts and other crops. He was born near Diamond Grove.

Dred Scott (circa 1795–1858) was a slave who sued his master to try to gain his freedom. He filed suit in the St. Louis Circuit Court. He lost his case in the U.S. Supreme Court.

Harry S. Truman (1884–1972) was the 33rd president of the United States (1945–1953). He was a U.S. senator from Missouri and served as vice president under President Franklin D. Roosevelt. He was born in Lamar.

Laura Ingalls Wilder (1867–1957) wrote the *Little House* books. Born in Wisconsin, she moved to Mansfield, Missouri, in 1894, where she wrote her books.

Jon Hamm (1971–) is an actor and TV director. He has won awards for his performance in the TV Show *Mad Men*. He was born in St. Louis.

Mark Twain (1835–1910) was a well-loved writer. His famous tales include *The Adventures of Tom Sawyer* and *The Adventures of Huckleberry Finn*. His real name was Samuel Langhorne Clemens.

STATE SYMBOLS

Tree

flowering dogwood

Flower

hawthorn

Bird

bluebird

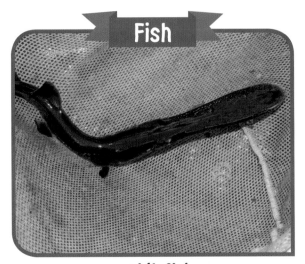

Fish

paddlefish

PebbleGo Next Bonus! To make an original Missouri dessert, go to www.pebblegonext.com and search keywords:

MO RECIPE

Fossil

crinoid

Horse

Missouri fox trotter

Musical Instrument

fiddle

Animal

Missouri mule

Insect

honeybee

Tree Nut

eastern black walnut

FAST FACTS

STATEHOOD
1821

CAPITAL ☆
Jefferson City

LARGEST CITY •
Kansas City

SIZE
68,742 square miles (178,041 square kilometers) land area
(2010 U.S. Census Bureau)

POPULATION
6,044,171 (2013 U.S. Census estimate)

STATE NICKNAME
Gateway to the West; Show-Me State

STATE MOTTO
"Salus Populi Suprema Lex Esto," which is Latin for "Let the welfare of
the people be the supreme law"

STATE SEAL

Missouri's state seal has two grizzly bears supporting a shield between them. The bears represent the state's strength and its citizens' bravery. The shield includes symbols of Missouri and of the United States. The left side of the shield has a bear and a crescent moon. The crescent moon represents Missouri's ability for growth. The U.S. coat of arms is on the shield's right side. The state motto, written in Latin, means "Let the welfare of the people be the supreme law." The motto lies on a scroll below the shield. The seal was adopted in 1822.

PebbleGo Next Bonus!
To print and color
your own flag, go to
www.pebblegonext.com
and search keywords:

MO FLAG

STATE FLAG

Missouri's flag was adopted in 1913. It has red, white, and blue stripes. In the center is a ring of 24 stars on a blue background. The stars symbolize that Missouri was the 24th state. The state seal lies within the ring of stars. Two grizzly bears stand on each side of the state seal. They stand for Missourians' strength and bravery. The bears hold a round shield. Around the shield is the motto "United We Stand, Divided We Fall." Beneath the bears' feet is the state motto in Latin.

MINING PRODUCTS

portland cement, limestone, lead, lime

MANUFACTURED GOODS

food products, chemicals, motor
vehicles and vehicle parts, machinery,
electrical equipment and appliances,
paper manufacturing

FARM PRODUCTS

beef, hogs, poultry, corn, hay, cotton,
soybeans, watermelons

PROFESSIONAL SPORTS TEAMS

Kansas City Chiefs (NFL)

Kansas City Royals (MLB)

Kansas City Wizards (MLS)

St. Louis Blues (NHL)

St. Louis Cardinals (MLB)

St. Louis Rams (NFL)

PebbleGo Next Bonus!
To learn the lyrics to
the state song, go to
www.pebblegonext.com
and search keywords:

MO SONG

MISSOURI TIMELINE

1600s The Sauk, Fox, Iowa, and Osage Indians live in Missouri.

1620 The Pilgrims establish a colony in the New World in present-day Massachusetts.

1673 French explorers Louis Jolliet and Jacques Marquette visit Missouri.

1682 Frenchman René-Robert Cavelier, known as Sieur de la Salle, claims a vast region for France. The land includes Missouri. The French name the area Louisiana.

1764 St. Louis is founded.

1803 The United States purchases the Louisiana Territory, which includes Missouri, from France.

1804 Meriwether Lewis and William Clark lead a group of explorers into the Louisiana Territory.

1811–1812 Earthquakes strike the Missouri area, destroying forests and sinking large areas of land.

1821 Missouri becomes the 24th state on August 10.

1838 Many Cherokee Indians pass through Missouri on their way to Indian Territory in present-day Oklahoma. The journey becomes known as the Trail of Tears, as the Cherokee suffer many hardships along the trail.

1861–1865 The Union and the Confederacy fight the Civil War. More than 100,000 Missouri men fight for the Union.

1875 A grasshopper infestation in Missouri causes an estimated $15 million in damage.

1904 St. Louis hosts the World's Fair.

1914–1918 World War I is fought; the United States enters the war in 1917.

1931 Bagnell Dam is built on the Osage River, creating the Lake of the Ozarks.

1945 Missourian Harry S. Truman becomes president of the United States.

1965 The Gateway Arch is completed in St. Louis, honoring St. Louis as the gateway to the West.

1993
The Missouri and Mississippi rivers overflow, creating serious floods that cause about $14 billion in damage.

2002
Tornadoes hit southeastern Missouri, destroying homes and businesses.

2011
A tornado strikes Joplin, killing more than 100 people, injuring more than 1,100 people, and causing major destruction.

2015
The Kansas City Royals win the World Series; it is their first championship title in 30 years.

Glossary

ethnicity *(ETH-niss-ih-tee)*—a group of people who share the same physical features, beliefs, and backgrounds

executive *(ig-ZE-kyuh-tiv)*—the branch of government that makes sure laws are followed

industry *(IN-duh-stree)*—a business which produces a product or provides a service

legislature *(LEJ-iss-lay-chur)*—a group of elected officials who have the power to make or change laws for a country or state

limestone *(LIME-stohn)*—hard rock used in building; made from the remains of ancient sea creatures

monument *(MON-yuh-muhnt)*—a statue or building that is meant to remind people of an event or a person

native *(NAY-tuhv)*—someone who originally lived in a certain place

region *(REE-juhn)*—a large area

saddlebag *(SAD-uhl-bag)*—one of a pair of bags that are laid across the back of a horse behind the saddle

sea level *(SEE LEV-uhl)*—the average level of the surface of the ocean, used as a starting point from which to measure the height or depth of any place

tourism *(TOOR-i-zuhm)*—the business of taking care of visitors to a country or place

Read More

Ganeri, Anita. *United States of America: A Benjamin Blog and His Inquisitive Dog Guide.* Country Guides. Chicago: Heinemann Raintree, 2015.

Koontz, Robin. *What's Great About Missouri?* Our Great States. Minneapolis: Lerner Publications, 2016.

Sanders, Doug. *Missouri.* It's My State! New York: Cavendish Square Publishing, 2016.

Internet Sites

FactHound offers a safe, fun way to find Internet sites related to this book. All of the sites on FactHound have been researched by our staff.

Here's all you do:

Visit *www.facthound.com*

Type in this code: 9781515704126

 Check out projects, games and lots more at
www.capstonekids.com

Critical Thinking Using the Common Core

1. Name two types of livestock that farmers raise in Missouri. (Key Ideas and Details)

2. The Pony Express was a mail service that ran from 1860 to 1861. Men rode horses carrying saddlebags of mail between St. Joseph, Missouri, and Sacramento, California. What challenges might the men have faced during their travels? (Integration of Knowledge and Ideas)

3. What year did Missouri become the 24th state? Hint: Use the timeline to help answer this question. (Craft and Structure)

Index